People of the Rain Forest

RAIN FORESTS TODAY

Ted O'Hare

An Embera Indian girl holds her brother at a village in Panama.

Rourke

Publishing LLC

Vero Beach, Florida 32964

www.rourkepublishing.com

PHOTO CREDITS: cover, title page, page 4 (inset), 7 (both), 8 (both), 10, 12,13 (inset) ©James H. Carmichael; all other photos ©Lynn Stone

Editor: Frank Sloan

Cover and page design by Nicola Stratford

Library of Congress Cataloging-in-Publication Data

O'Hare, Ted, 1961-
  People of the rain forest / Ted O'Hare.
     p. cm. — (Rain forests today)
  Includes bibliographical references and index.
  ISBN 1-59515-153-2 (hardcover)
 1. Rain forest people--Juvenile literature. 2. Rain forests--Juvenile literature. 3. Rain forest ecology--Juvenile literature. I. Title. II. Series: O'Hare, Ted, 1961- Rain forests today.
  GN394.O37 2004
  306'.09152--dc22   2004006197

Printed in the USA

CG/CG

Table of Contents

A boy walks on stilts through his rain forest village in Panama.

People in the Forest

Tropical rain forests are warm, wet, and wild. Many **species**, or kinds, of plants and animals live there. The largest rain forests are found in South America, Southeast Asia, and West Africa. But there are rain forests in many other places.

Rain forests are also home for people. These people have lived in rain forests for hundreds or even thousands of years.

The lush, green rain forests of the world are home for countless kinds of plants and animals.

Tribal People

Many **tribal** people still live in rain forests. They eat monkeys, jungle birds, the honey from wild bees, and whatever else they can find. They use wood and leaves to build their homes.

Some tribal people farm at least some of the time. They grow bananas, peppers, cotton, and squash.

More than half the species of plants and animals in the world are found in tropical rain forests.

A dugout canoe hauls bananas from one rain forest village to another in Peru.

This Embera girl lives
in tropical Panama.

A Kuna Indian woman in Panama opens a coconut.

Living in the Rain Forest

Native people respect the forest. They change only what they need to change. They clear just enough land to grow crops. Or they clear no land at all.

Forest tribes often move from one part of the rain forest to another. Soon the forest grows again over ground they may have cleared.

A native home stands along a river bank in tropical Peru.

Dangers to Living

Tropical rain forests provide food, shelter, and **medicine**. These are all basic needs.

Governments sometimes decide to clear rain forests. This brings danger to the peoples' **traditional** way of living. The tribal peoples don't know any other way of life. They may be forced to move elsewhere.

Large cut-and-burn projects can destroy ways of life as well as rain forests.

Destroying the Rain Forests

There are many reasons for governments to destroy the rain forests. The **lumber** that comes from trees is very valuable. Cleared land can be used for farming or for building.

Beef cattle graze on cleared rain forest land in Costa Rica.

New roads open rain forest
villages to change.

Farmers raise cattle on land that was once rain forests. They can also plant crops, such as coffee, tea, pineapple, bananas, and **papayas**. Governments need to decide how much land they should clear. They also need to decide how much land should be left alone.

Banana trees grow at the cleared edge of a Central American rain forest.

Visitors to Rain Forests

People come from many places to see the tropical rain forests. Scientists go there to study. They want to find new plants and animals. They want to know how the rain forest "works" and what lives there.

Some people come just to see the wonders of the rain forest.

A biologist hiking in the rain forest spies an anole lizard.

Discoveries in the Rain Forest

Long ago, tribal people found plants that were good to eat. They also discovered plants that helped them cure diseases.

Scientists today are still making new discoveries. Some scientists are learning how the tribal people use plants as medicine.

About 100 plants are now used to make different kinds of medicine.

A German scientist studies mushrooms at a field station in the Central American rain forest.

Rain Forest Life

Scientists are working hard to identify the huge numbers of plant and animal species. This is because so much of the rain forest is being destroyed. Scientists want to see new species before they are destroyed or become **extinct**.

Some scientists think there may even be 30 million or more kinds of insects. So far, fewer than 1 million have been identified.

A scientist reaches with her collecting wand to lift a small lizard from a rain forest vine.

A scientist at La Selva uses high-tech equipment to study the rain forest.

La Selva

One of the best known places for rain forest study is in Costa Rica. It is the La Selva Biological Research Station. This is a modern **laboratory** in the middle of the rain forest.

Scientists there learn about the way in which plants, animals, air, soil, and water work together. What scientists learn can help governments make wise decisions about the future of the world's tropical rain forests.

Glossary

extinct (EK stinkt) — no longer existing

laboratory (LAB uh ruh tore ee) — a place where scientists study

lumber (LUHM bur) — wood used in the building process

medicine (MED uh sen) — a substance used to treat disease

native (NAY tihv) — found naturally in an area

papayas (puh PIE yuhs) — edible fruit from the tropical papaya tree

species (SPEE sheez) — a certain kind of plant or animal within a closely related group

traditional (truh DISH en ul) — something possessing long-held traditions

tribal (TRY bul) — referring to a group of people who live in a tribe

Index

Further Reading

Castner, James L. *Native Peoples*. Benchmark Books, 2001.
Low, Robert. *Peoples of the Rain Forest*. Rosen, 2003.
Woods, Mae. *People of the Rain Forest*. Abdo & Daughters, 1999.

Websites to Visit

www.junglephotos.com/
www.ran.org/kidscorner/
www.pbs.org/wgbh/nova/shaman/shaman.html

About the Author

Ted O'Hare is an author and editor of children's nonfiction books. He divides his time between New York City and a home upstate.